Adoniram Judson Eaton

Latin Prose Exercises Based upon Livy, Book XXI

And Selections for Translation into Latin, with Parallel Passages from Livy

Adoniram Judson Eaton

Latin Prose Exercises Based upon Livy, Book XXI
And Selections for Translation into Latin, with Parallel Passages from Livy

ISBN/EAN: 9783337078225

Printed in Europe, USA, Canada, Australia, Japan

Cover: Foto ©Thomas Meinert / pixelio.de

More available books at **www.hansebooks.com**

LATIN PROSE EXERCISES

BASED UPON

LIVY, BOOK XXI.,

AND

SELECTIONS FOR TRANSLATION INTO LATIN,

WITH PARALLEL PASSAGES FROM LIVY.

BY

A. JUDSON EATON, PH.D. (LEIPZIG),

McGILL UNIVERSITY, MONTREAL.

BOSTON, U.S.A., AND LONDON:
PUBLISHED BY GINN & COMPANY.
1898.

TYPOGRAPHY BY J. S. CUSHING & CO., BOSTON, U.S.A.

PRESSWORK BY GINN & CO., BOSTON, U.S.A.

PREFACE.

———◦◦———

IT is generally conceded that the best way of study-
ing Latin prose is in connection with the reading of
Latin authors. The translation of the Latin is in this
way done with more care, thought, and appreciation;
the desired grammatical drill is acquired, as well as, in
addition to a vocabulary, a precise and definite sense of
Latin style.

Our great models for Latin prose are Caesar, Cicero,
and Livy. Of exercises based upon Caesar's Commen-
taries, we have no lack. But in beginning the reading
of Livy, similar lessons were unknown to the author, and
the following exercises were prepared, based upon the
twenty-first book, as preliminary to Latin composition
after the style of Livy.

Short oral exercises are recommended in connection
with the translation of each chapter, and after a thorough study of several chapters, in which each word,
phrase, construction, and arrangement have been carefully noted, the written exercises are to be taken up.
At first close imitation is exacted, till the learner gets
into the swing of the author's style. Then follow exer-

cises, graduated in difficulty, of a more complex and less literal character, and extracts from leading historians, parallel to some extent, in subject and style, to portions of Livy, already read.

After the completion of the twenty-first book; composition exercises are continued in connection with sight-reading. The rhetorical stories of Livy are often short and complete in themselves, so that they can be read fairly well by the help of a brief introduction. After a selection has been read at sight, the student may be requested to study it more minutely, and then a suitable extract, similar in manner and style, may be put into his hands for translation. A few such passages, with notes subjoined, have been added.

On questions of grammar, references are given to Allen and Greenough's Latin Grammar (A. & G.), and Harkness' Latin Grammar (H.). In an appendix will be found suggestions to students, notes on idioms, and a study of the periodic style of Livy; references to which are made by sections (§). In the preparation of these notes, considerable indebtedness is due to Potts' admirable work *Hints towards Latin Prose Composition*, and Postgate's *Sermo Latinus*, a short guide to Latin prose composition.

A. J. E.

McGILL UNIVERSITY,
Sept. 7, 1891.

LATIN PROSE EXERCISES.

LIVY, BOOK XXI.

I. — Chaps. 1 and 2.

By way of introduction[1] to this division of my work, I may[2] state that I am about to describe the most famous war ever waged, namely, that which the Carthaginians, under the leadership[3] of Hannibal, maintained with the Roman people.[4] No other[5] states which have waged war against one another ever had so great resources[6] or power or strength, as Rome[7] and Carthage[7] at that time. The war was carried on[8] with intense hatred on both sides, but especially on the part of the Carthaginians, because the conquered had been subjected[9] to an imperious and rapacious exercise[1] of authority.

Hamilcar, the father of Hannibal, a man of high spirit, had been galled[8] by the loss[10] of Sardinia and Sicily ; and with good reason, for[11] Roman fraud[12] had snatched them from Carthage, during the African mutiny. Had he lived[13] longer, it is clear that the Carthaginians led by him would have entered Italy in arms.

[1] § 1. Render here by **praefāri**. [2] Use **licet**. For Const., see A. & G. 227. e., 331. i. Note 3. H. 538. [3] Abl. Abs. A. & G. 255. a. H. 431. 4. § 17. [4] A. & G. 344. k. [5] Not to be translated. [6] Distinguish in meaning between **vīs, rōbur, opēs**. Consult Lat.-Eng. Dict. [7] § 17. [8] § 16. [9] Use **imperō**. What mood? A. & G. 321. a., 230. H. 516. II., 301. 1: [10] A. & G. 292. a. § 19. [11] *and with good reasons, for :* **namque**, a strengthened **nam** (cf. καὶ γάρ). See Lat.-Eng. Dict. [12] Means. [13] A. & G. 308, 337. b. H. 510, 527. Study also A. &. G. 343–345. H. 560–569.

II. — Chaps. 2 and 3.

Hamilcar's death delayed the war, and during an interval of about [1] eight years, between the demise of the father and succession of the son, the supreme command was held by Hasdrubal, who had won in early youth the favor of Hamilcar.   Hasdrubal, a statesman rather than a general,[2] advanced the Carthaginian interests [3] far more by forming friendly alliances with neighboring chiefs than his father-in-law had by force [4] of arms.   For he had a wonderful tact in winning over new tribes, and in dealing with petty chiefs.   He was assassinated [5] in open day by a barbarian, B.C. 221.[6]   The soldiers instantly carried Hannibal into the general's tent and proclaimed him commander-in-chief amid loud and universal [7] acclamation.   Now Hannibal hated Rome most of all.[8]   For when he was a small boy, about nine years old, his father, who chanced [9] to be sacrificing before transporting his army to Spain, had set [10] the child before the altar, and with his hand upon the victim, made him swear [11] eternal [12] enmity to Rome.

[1] Distinguish **ferē, fermē, paene,** and **prope.**   [2] See " Suggestions," 10.   [3] See "Suggestions," 10.   [4] Hendiadys, § 13.   [5] § 16. [6] Use the Roman method of reckoning time.   [7] *Universal :* **omnium.** § 9.   [8] Render by one word.   [9] Use **fŏrte.**   [10] Use the participial const.   Remember that the Latin prefers subordination, English co-ordination of clauses.   § 21.   [11] *made swear :* consult Dict. under **adīgō.**   [12] Distinguish between **perpetuus, aeternus, sempiternus.**

III. — Chaps. 1-5.

Now that Hannibal held the supreme command, through the influence of the Barcine faction, his actions[1] soon showed plainly that he was destined to become a great general. Sent[2] to Spain, he at once attracted the admiration of the entire army. The esteem of the old soldiers was further won by his father's memory. [3] "Can this," said they, "be Hamilcar, restored to us again in his youth[4]?" They saw in him the same features, the same animated look and penetrating eye, the same high spirit and bitter hatred of the Roman. Naturally fearless and with confidence in his own powers, with a temper adapted[5] to obey as well as to command, he was beloved by all. He could[6] endure any labor; and whatever time was left to him after business was finished he gave to repose; yet he would[7] lie, not on a soft couch, but on the bare ground, among the guards, wrapped in his military cloak.

Many historians have falsely ascribed[8] to Carthage's greatest general[9] inhuman cruelty and perfidiousness, affirming[10] that he had no regard for the truth, no sense of religion.

[1] § 1. [2] A. & G. 292. H. 549. [3] A. & G. 338. H. 523. [4] A. & G. 186. c. H. 443. [5] **habilis**: A. & G. 299, and footnote; 234. b; 300. H. 391. [6] § 5. [7] A. & G. 277. H. 469. § 5. [8] *falsely ascribed:* **falsō insimulāre.** [9] § 10. [10] A. & G. 336. 2, N. 2.

IV. — Chaps. 1-6.

In resolving on war in Spain in order to rouse the Romans to arms,[1] Hannibal was but carrying out[2] the original design[3] of his father, whose actions[4] showed[5] plainly that he was meditating a greater war than that in which he was engaged. But he had been cut[6] off by a premature[7] death. Hasdrubal, too, had been murdered in open day by a barbarian : and now, for fear[8] that some[9] accident might, if he hesitated,[10] cut short his career[11] also,[12] [13] Hannibal thought that there must not be a moment's delay. He determined to provoke Rome to arms by an attack on her allies, the Saguntines, and stormed and plundered the city of Cartala, the rich capital of the Alcades. He laid waste the country round about,[14] and soon all beyond the Ebro, except Saguntum, was in Carthaginian hands. And now, that it might seem that he had been drawn into the attack upon the Saguntines by the course of events, the neighboring tribes were made to pick a quarrel with them, while he espoused the cause of the former.

[1] Latin idiom, *Roman arms.* [2] **exsequor.** [3] *original design:* render this idea by a verb and adverb. § 1. [4] Employ **sē gerere.** §§ 1, 17. [5] What mood ? A. & G. 319. H. 500. [6] **opprimō.** [7] **immātūrus.** Consult Lat.-Eng. Dict. [8] *for fear that:* **nē.** A. & G. 331 f. H. 498. III. [9] A. & G. 105 d. H. 190. 1. [10] A. & G. 292. H. 549. [11] §§ 17. 1. "Suggestions," 10. [12] A. & G. 345. b. H. 569. III. [13] Before translating the following sentences, consult §§ 21-23. [14] Render by an adjective.

V. — Chaps. 1-6.

War was not yet openly declared, but there were already grounds for it. [1]The Saguntines saw that they were threatened with immediate danger, and despatched ambassadors to Rome, [2]imploring assistance. The matter was brought before the senate, [3]in the consulship of Publius Scipio and Tiberius Longus, 219 B.C., and it[4] was decided to send ambassadors into Spain [5]with instructions to investigate the condition of their allies, [4]and, if they saw sufficient reason, to warn Hannibal no[.] to meddle with the Saguntines, as being allies of Rome. But before the embassy had been despatched,[6] news of the siege came unexpectedly,[7] and all Rome was fired with indignation,[8] that the conquered should [9]presume to attack the allies of the Roman people. The question of public policy was again[10] brought before the senate, and a second motion[11] prevailed that the commission should proceed [12]to Carthage in Africa to insist upon the surrender of the general's person.[13]

[1] Latin idiom: *the Saguntines, when they saw.* § 23. d. [2] In how many ways might this be expressed? A. & G. 318. [3] Adverbial phrases of *time* usually stand at the beginning of a sentence. [4] How best translated? A. & G. 180. f., 201. e. § 14. [5] *with instructions to:* ut. [6] Abl. Abs. A. & G. 255. H. 431. [7] I.e. *sooner than the hope of all.* A. & G. 247. b. H. 417. N. 5. [8] **indignor.** What two constructions may this verb take after it? A. & G. 333. b. H. 535. III. [9] **ūltrō ĭnferre:** *presume to attack.* Consult Lat.-Eng. Dict. under **ūltrō.** [10] Distinguish between **ĭterum, rūrsus, dēnuō** (dē novō). [11] **sententĭa.** [12] A. & G. 259. h. [13] **ĭpse.**

VI. — Chaps. 1-12.

Now [1]while the Romans were wasting their time in
discussing the situation,[2] Hannibal had already begun
the attack on Saguntum with the greatest energy.[3]
This city, which stood at the distance of one mile from
the sea,[4]abounded in wealth, and had grown up to such a
degree of opulence that it was by far the most important
of any beyond the Ebro. [5]Thinking that its possession
would [6]be invaluable to him, and any delay imprudent,
he marched into their territory, in three divisions. He
then surrounded the city with his engines, [7]and batter-
ing-rams were advanced up to the walls. The townsmen
defended themselves with great vigor, and at first kept
off the enemy with missiles, while Hannibal himself,
ever the foremost in advancing to the fight, was severely
wounded in the thigh. In consequence of this, there
was a cessation of arms for a few days, while the general's wound [8]was healing, though there[9] was no inter-
mission of the preparations.

[1] A. & G. 328. a.   H. 467. 4.   [2] "Suggestions," 10.   [8] A. & G.
248. II. 419. III.   [4] *abounded in wealth :* transl. by the superlative of the adjective.   [5] **ratus.**   A. & G. 290. b. H. 550. N.
[6] **māximī esse mōmentī.**   [7] Abl. Abs.   [8] What mood ? A. & G.
328. H. 519.   [9] Impersonal construction.

VII. — Chaps. 1-12.

After the general's wound had been healed,[1] the contest began anew with greater fury. The battering-ram was applied at a number of points, [2]and the walls in many places were shattered. [3]Three towers in one range, together with the whole stretch of wall between them, had been battered down by the engines[4]; when, [5]as if the wall had served for a covering to both armies alike, [6]besiegers and besieged rushed[7] through the breach. Here the fortune of war was changeful and uncertain; [8]the courage of both was animated [9]to the highest pitch : on the one side by hope, on the other by despair. The townsmen, finding that they had succeeded beyond expectation, and trusting to their valor, suddenly raised[10] a shout, rushed[10] from all parts into the breach, and drove[10] the enemy off. There was consternation and panic everywhere, and they fled in disorder to their camps.

[1] What mood and tense? A. & G. 324. H. 518. [2] Note the relation between the members of this sentence. "Suggestions," 3. § 21. [3] See preceding note. Consult also A. & G. 325. b. [4] tormentum. [5] A. & G. 312. H. 513. II. [6] "Suggestions," 10. [7] § 16. [8] "Suggestions," 10. [9] summē. [10] A. & G. 276. d. H. 467. III.

VIII. — Chaps. 1-12.

At this crisis, it was announced that ambassadors
[1] from Rome had arrived [2] to represent the complaints of
the Saguntines. [3] Hannibal forthwith sent messengers
to the seashore to meet them [4] and to say that he had no
time to listen to embassies. At the same time he despatched letters beforehand to Carthage, knowing well
that the Roman ambassadors, [5] being refused a hearing,
would go straight [6] to Carthage. [7] Hanno was the leader
of the party opposed to the Barcine faction, and [8] made
a long speech [9] before the senate. A few concurred in
opinion with Hanno, who pleaded for the treaty, and
feared that this little fire which Hannibal was kindling
might some day blaze forth into a mighty conflagration.
[10] "Your armies," said he, "are besieging Saguntum,
which a treaty forbids you to touch; before long Rome's
legions will be besieging Carthage. That enemy has
been tested in the first Punic war; of Rome's power you
are not altogether ignorant. The claims of her envoys
for satisfaction are in accordance with the treaty, and
I for my part maintain that we ought to grant what
they ask."

[1] I.e. Roman ambassadors. § 9. [2] Render by a rel. cl. [3] "Suggestions," 3. [4] *and to say :* purpose. [5] **nōn admissōs.** [6] **rēctā.**
A. & G. 258. g. H. 420. 3. [7] Combine the following two sentences.
§ 21. [8] **longam ōrātiōnem habuit.** [9] **apud** (or **adversus**)
senātum. [10] Employ indirect narration.

IX. — Chaps. 1-12.

Meanwhile [1] the Carthaginian general gave his soldiers a few days' [2] rest, and by a liberal distribution of money, and by publicly proclaiming that the spoils of the captured city should belong to the soldiers, kindled their ardor.[3] The Saguntines, [4] on the other hand, wearied as they were with fighting, worked night and day without cessation [5] in rebuilding the city walls. [6] Hannibal's departure on an expedition against two tribes, who had caused some apprehension of a revolt, had revived their sinking spirits for a while. But on his return [5] an assault fiercer than ever, directed by Hannibal in person,[7] had to be faced by the citizens. He pressed the attack so vigorously that, after great slaughter on both sides, part of the citadel itself was taken. Much credit [8] was given to Maharbal, who had been left in command by Hannibal, had fought several successful engagements, and had demolished a good part of the walls.

---

[1] "Suggestions," 10.　　[2] A. & G. 215. b.　H. 390. V.　[3] § 17.
[4] autem.　A. & G. 345. b.　H. 569. III.　[5] § 1.　[6] A. & G. 344. d.
H. 561. I.　[7] ipse.　[8] in honōre māgnō esse.

X. — Chaps. 1-18.

[1]A few on both sides still had a little hope of peace, and tried to realize it. Alorcus, a Spaniard, the recognized guest and friend of the Saguntines, offered to be the negotiator of a peace. [2]He crossed the line, and had an interview before the senate. [3] "I bring," [4]said he [5]at the close of a long speech, "terms of a peace, inevitable rather than favorable, for everything belongs to the victor. So long as your strength held out,[6] or you hoped[6] for aid from Rome, I never[7] mentioned [4]peace to you. Grievous and hard though the terms are, yet I maintain that it is advisable that you should endure them rather than see your wives and children seized and dragged into slavery. Listen,[8] then, to the terms Hannibal grants, and for my part I do not despair of some mitigation of them." He gave them good counsel, but,[9] as often happens, without winning any one to his side. [10]While he was yet speaking, a report spread throughout the city that Hannibal was making an attack in full force, and had given a cruel order for the massacre of all the adult males.

[1] § 21. [2] Subordinate by using the participle. [3] Use indirect narration. [4] A. & G. 336. 2, 336. A. H. 523. [5] *at the close of a long speech:* translated by one word. [6] A. & G. 336. 2, 336. B. H. 524. [7] Render by **nec unquam.** The negative when emphatic begins the Latin sentence. A. & G. 345. d. H. 569. IV. [8] A. & G. 339. H. 523. II. [9] *but without winning.* For the different ways in which *without,* followed by a verbal noun, is rendered in Latin (since the preposition **sine** is never used with the gerund), see Madvig, § 417. Obs. 3. Here a copulative conjunction may be used: **neque tamen.** [10] What mood? A. & G. 327. H. 520.

XI.—Chaps. 1-18.

At length the town was taken, after an eight months'[1] siege. Though all[2] of the gold and silver belonging to the state and individuals had been collected and flung into the fire kindled for that purpose, still an immense booty was taken, and the victorious army, laden with spoil, retired into winter quarters at New Carthage.[3]

Hannibal's object[4] had been attained[5]: [6]no longer could war be averted. [7]The influence of the Barcine faction was dominant[8] at home ; the senate was devoted to him ; and though they listened to Hanno in a speech more bitter than the denunciations of the Roman ambassadors, it was not with approval. The reply was that the war had been begun by the Saguntines, not by Hannibal. [9]They had first fomented disputes between the neighboring tribes. Thus the mission of the envoys to Carthage proved fruitless. They returned to Rome [10]with the information that everything tended to war.

[1] Translate *in the eighth month after*, etc. See also A. & G. 143. a. H. 297. 1. [2] An attributive adjective belonging to several nouns is generally expressed only once, and agrees with the noun nearest to itself. H. 439. 1. [3] A. & G. 259. b. [4] Employ the verb **petō**. [5] **cōnsequor.** Distinguish **cōnsequor, nancīscor, adipīscor.** See page 29, note 9. [6] "Suggestions," 3. [7] § 17. What would naturally be the subject in Latin ? [8] **plūrimum valēre.** [9] A. & G. 336. 2. a. 1. [10] I.e. *and reported.*

XII.—Chaps. 1-18.

When it was reported[1] at Rome that Saguntum had
fallen, the people were seized[2] with sorrow for the [3]loss
of their allies and with shame for having neglected them.
The fathers were apprehensive for the [4]public safety;
but they were so distracted by varied emotions at the
same time that there was more confusion than counsel
among them. All were of opinion, however, that the
war should be at once carried on by land and sea, [5]and
that most vigorously. [6]The provinces were assigned to
the consuls of the year. Spain fell to the lot of Cornelius, Africa to Sempronius. The forces were divided
between the consuls: of Romans and allies there were
enrolled [7]64,000 infantry and [7]6200 cavalry. The foe
they had to encounter was more warlike than any previ-
ous one. For twenty-three years the Carthaginian army
had been trained under a determined and indefatigable
leader, and had been uniformly successful in [8]campaigns
of severest fighting in Spain.

[1] A. & G. 330. a. b.   H. 534. 1.   [2] § 16.   [3] I.e. *for their allies lost.*
A. & G. 217, 292. a.   H. 396. III., 549. 5. N. 2.   § 19.   [4] **Summa
rērum** denotes *general welfare, public safety, general interest,
existence of the state.* What construction may **summa** take here ?
A. & G. 217. c.   H. 396. III. N.   [5] *and that :* omit in translation
and express their force by the arrangement of words.   [6] Combine
this sentence with the following by using *one* predicate.   [7] A. & G.
94. e.   H. 178. If there is added to the thousands a lower declina-
ble number, then the objects numbered, if they are placed after,
stand in the same case as **mīlia**: e.g. **tria mīlia (et) trecentī
mīlitēs caesī sunt**; otherwise in the genitive pl. ; as, **tria mīlia
mīlitum et trecentī caesī sunt**; or, **caesa sunt mīlitum tria
mīlia trecentī.**   [8] **mīlitia.**

XIII. — Chaps. 1-18.

Yet war was not [1] at once declared. The question was submitted to the people, whether [2] they wished that a second [3] embassy be sent to Carthage [4] to find out whether [2] Hannibal had attacked Saguntum by order of the state or [5] had laid siege to it of his own accord. To the Roman envoys, when admitted to an audience, this reply was given: [6] "The question ought not to be whether the state or a private individual was responsible for the attack upon Saguntum, but whether the attack was just or unjust. The treaty with Rome has in no way been violated, for in that treaty no provision was made for Saguntum. Moreover, the Carthaginians ought certainly not to be bound by the treaty of Hasdrubal, which he made without their consent. Did not your senate say that you could not accept the treaty which Caius Lutatius, your consul, first made with us, because it was made without your full sanction and consent?"

[7] Thereupon the Roman gathered his robe into a fold, and said: "Here we bring peace or war: take which you please." Amid loud and universal acclamation, instantly came the reply: "Give which you please." The Roman shook out his fold and spoke again: "I give you war."

[1] *at once:* **prōtinus.** [2] A. & G. 211, 334. H. 353, 529. [3] Employ the adverb. [4] A. & G. 318. [5] "Suggestions," 10. [6] Use indirect narration. A. & G. 336, 338. H. 523, 524, 529. [7] Commit to memory in Latin Livy's description of this scene.

XIV. — Chaps. 1-20.

When the war was finished in Africa,[1] the Romans
fraudulently seized Sardinia, and imposed a war tribute
on Carthage. About the same time the loss of Sicily
sorely[2] vexed[3] a high-spirited[4] people, and[5] the Carthaginians determined on war. First they attacked Rome's[6]
allies in Spain,[7] who vigorously undertook their own
defence in the hope of aid from Rome.[7] But in vain[8];
their chief city fell after a siege[9] of eight months,[10] and
orders were given for the massacre[11] of all the adult
males.   Terror-stricken by this[12] calamity,[13] the neighboring tribes submitted, believing that they had been
cruelly betrayed by their Roman allies,[13] and that they
could no longer trust to Roman faith. Mingled shame
and fear[11] took possession of the hearts of the Romans;
war was forthwith declared and troops levied; while
ambassadors were sent to visit the states in Spain to
win them over to an alliance with Rome.[7] Save that
they were received and heard, no friendly answer was
received, until[14] they came to Marseilles. With the information there acquired, the envoys returned home,
where they found the whole city excited by its anticipa-
tions of war.

[1] I.e. *African war.* § 9. [2] *sorely:* the force of the English
adverb is often contained in the verbal idea. [3] A. & G. 344. d.
H. 561. I. [4] A. & G. 215. H. 396. V. [5] Note the force of the connective here. "Suggestions," 3. [6] I.e. *allies of the Roman people.*
§ 17. [7] Phrases formed with prepositions are used in Latin chiefly
as adverbial equivalents; rarely as adjective equivalents. [8] Distinguish between **frūstrā** and **nec quicquam.** [9] Employ the verb
oppūgnārī. § 1.   Consult also A. & G. 143. a. H. 297. t. [10] § 21.
[11] § 1.   [12] § 14.   [13] A. & G. 209. b. H. 569. IV. 1. [14] A. & G.
262, 327. H. 520.

XV. — Chaps. 19-25.

[*Before writing this exercise, turn Hannibal's Vision, ch. 22, into Direct Discourse, and commit to memory. Study in connection, A. & G. 336–342; H. 523–529.*]

[1]From Carthage, the embassy passed over to Spain and Gaul, [2]to attempt to win them over to an alliance with Rome. After making a circuit of both states [3]without effecting anything, they returned to Rome. The Roman request,[4] that the Gauls should refuse the right of way through their territory, [5]if the Carthaginian[6] tried[7] to invade Italy, was greeted with laughter and a general cry of displeasure. [8]Never had they received any kindness from Rome[9]; on the contrary, heavy tributes had been imposed upon them, and [10]they had been subjected to indignities[4] of every kind. Why, then, should they be so foolish as to turn the war upon themselves, [11]instead of allowing it to pass into Italy, and expose their own lands [12]to devastation instead of those of strangers? Their unfavorable reception[4] was due to the fact that the ruins of Saguntum was a melancholy and forcible warning to the states of Spain; and that the minds of the Gauls were already prepossessed in favor of Hannibal, and that the attachment of many of their chiefs had been secured through gold.

[1] §§ 21, 22, 23. [2] A. & G. 317. H. 497. [3] See Ex. X. N. 9. [4] § 1. [5] A. & G. 276. b, 292. H. 549. 2. [6] "Suggestions," 10. [7] § 3. [8] Indirect Narration. [9] § 17. [10] Turn, 'they had suffered every indignity.' [11] Render by a negative purpose clause. [12] A. & G. 294. d. H. 544. 2. N. 2.

XVI. —Chaps. 19-25.

As we have before remarked, Hannibal, [1]after the capture of Saguntum, had retired into winter quarters at New Carthage. He also gave leave of absence to his Spanish soldiers to return home to visit their friends,[2] if they chose, since they might soon be called to service far away from their homes.

[3]Early in the spring, Hannibal [4]broke up his camp, and led his men [5]along the coast, as far as the Ebro. For the protection of Spain, 12,000 infantry, 1500 cavalry, and nearly half the elephants were left behind: [6]the chief command and the government of Spain being intrusted to Hannibal's younger[7] brother Hasdrubal. With the main[8] army he determined to invade Italy, and crossed the Ebro. Arrived at the Pyrenees, Hannibal sent home a portion of his troops, whom he perceived weary of the service, and he hoped thereby to inspire his army with greater confidence, even pretending that the Carpetani, who had left him, had been dismissed by his own act. He then crossed the Pyrenees with 50,000 infantry and 9000 cavalry.

[1] Abl. Abs.   [2] Omit *friends*.   A. & G. 197. d.   H. 441.   [3] A. & G. 193. H. 440. N. 1.   [4] *to break up camp:* castra movēre. What construction here ?   [5] What case ?   A. & G. 258. g.   H. 420. 1. 3).   [6] Render *to Hasdrubal as commander-in-chief*, etc.   [7] A. & G. 91. c., 253.   [8] Consult Lat.-Eng. Dict. under summa.

XVII. — Chaps. 26–32.

Passage of the Rhone.

[1]At the end of July, B.C. 218, the Carthaginian army arrived at the Rhone, where Hannibal found[2] the further bank occupied by the armed Volcae. [3]All the other tribes he had bribed into submission. [4]While rafts were being constructed for use on the spot and others collected from all sides, Hanno, son of Bomilcar, with part of the army proceeded up the stream. When a suitable point was reached, they crossed the river in hastily constructed boats, with a view of taking the Gauls in the rear. On the following day the smoke-signals showed that they had succeeded in crossing; [5]and seeing these, Hannibal gave the order to advance. [4]While the Gauls were engaged in a terrible conflict on the shore, Hanno had taken their camp, and was now pressing them on their rear. Beset[6] on either side with peril, they fled in confusion to their villages. Scipio, who had been despatched from Rome with sixty ships of war, encamped at the mouth of the Rhone, while a picked body of cavalry might reconnoitre the country. But finding that Hannibal was already too far ahead to be easily overtaken, he returned to Genua,[7] to encounter Hannibal, [8]on his descent from the Alps.

---

[1] **Extrēmō mēnse Iūliō.** [2] Distinguish **invenīre** and **reperīre**.
[3] Combine with the preceding. § 21. [4] A. & G. 276. e. H. 467. 4.
[5] A. & G. 180. f. H. 453. § 14. [6] **circumveniō.** [7] A. & G.
293 b, 318. d. H. 549. 3. [8] I.e. *descending.* A. & G. 292. H. 549. I.

XVIII. — Chaps. 31–38.

PASSAGE OF THE ALPS.

(a) Hannibal continued his march up the bank of the river and to the passes of the Alps without any molestation from the inhabitants of these regions. On the fourth day, he arrived among the Allobroges, who inhabited a plain called the "Island," between the Rhone and Isère. Here he dextrously[1] availed[2] himself of a feud that had [3]broken out between two brothers, who were contending for the throne, to [4]render assistance to the elder, who on this account supplied him with provisions, arms, and clothing. [5]When the army reached the foot of the Alps, scenes too horrible to describe revived their terror; and the expedition narrowly escaped destruction at the crossing of the first Alpine pass and one of the narrowest. [6]The natives had strongly beset the pass; and as the vanguard was struggling up the lower heights, they suddenly rushed out to the attack. Hannibal ordered a halt, and encamped[7] at the foot of the mountain,[8] until after sunset, when the Celts dispersed[9] to their various homes. Then taking with him brave[10] and picked men he seized the heights in the night.

---

[1] callidē.   [2] *avail one's self of:* ūtor.   [3] exorior.   [4] subvenio.   [5] § 16.   [6] How connected with the preceding sentence? [7] *at the foot of:* sub.   [8] A. & G. 328.   H. 519.   [9] Mood and tense? [10] § 15.

(*b*) At length, on the ninth day, the summit was gained.[1] The soldiers were now wellnigh [2]worn out by the incessant[3] attacks of the mountaineers, and here they were allowed to rest. On the second day, however, they broke up camp and began to advance. But the descent was much more difficult than the ascent had been, for the path was extremely steep, and the men could scarcely keep themselves from falling on the smooth and slippery ice : men and beasts oft were precipitated into the chasms. And now when all were exhausted by ceaseless exertion, and despair was visibly written [4]on every face, they pitched their camp on a mountain height, which commanded a wide and distant view[5] of the plains around the Po, of valleys and sunny hills, too, fit[6] to be the habitations of men. [7]In the next three days, they reached level ground. The passage of the Alps had consumed fifteen days. It is not known how large a force Hannibal had when he arrived in Italy. The statement[8] in the speech of Scipio that he had lost two-thirds of his cavalry and infantry with which he crossed the Ebro is without doubt[9] an exaggeration.[10]

[1] § 16. A. & G. 146. d. H. 301. 1. [2] See Ex. II. N. 1. [3] **assi-duus** or **continuus**. [4] Employ **ēmineō**, or change the form of expression: *all had come to the height of despair.* [5] § 1. [6] **idō-neus**. A. & G. 234. b. H. 391. I. II. [7] A. & G. 259. c. H. 429. [8] § 1. [9] Best expressed also by a verb: **dubitārī nōn potest.** A. & G. 332. g. H. 504. 3. 2). [10] **mālus vērō.**

XIX.

[Before doing this exercise, study carefully Chaps. 40 and 41, reading them in Indirect Narration. Study in connection, A. & G. 336–342; H. 523–529.]

The two armies met in the plain between the Ticino and the Sesia; and Scipio, [1]before leading his men into action, encouraged his soldiers by telling them that they were about to engage an enemy previously defeated and exhausted by their late[2] sufferings.[3] Two-thirds of their infantry had been lost in the passage over the Alps, while the condition[4] of the survivors was indescribably wretched.[5] [6]" But why," said he, " do I mention[7] these things ? The nature of the war is such that it ought especially to arouse and inflame your minds. We call[8] gods and men to witness that we have taken up arms that our persons may be safe from wrong. [9]At stake, too, is the safety of our friends and allies. Rome and the whole of Italy are compelled by the magnitude of the danger to [10]look for your aid. The gods themselves, who have been grievously wronged, will fitly punish the perfidious race. This is the same foe that you lately conquered by sea and land, [11]who sued for peace, which you granted, and which now they have broken by [12]this unprovoked attack."

[1] A. &. G. 327. H. 520. [2] **recēns**. [3] **calamitās**. [4] § 17. [5] Express by a verb, as, **suprā quam ēnarrārī possit**. [6] Employ Indirect Narration. [7] A. & G. 338. H. 523. II. [8] **testārī**. [9] *to be at stake* is **agī**. [10] **exspectāre**. [11] Combine the two rel. clauses. [12] **ūltrō**.

XX.—Chaps. 39, 45, 46.

Conflict on the Ticinus.

Though Hannibal had left Scipio in Gaul, he was now confronted by the same Roman commander, [1]as he descended into Italy. Scipio had already crossed the Po, and moved his camp to the river Ticinus, so that the two armies were in sight of each other. After words of encouragement on the part of the leaders, both sides [2]prepared for battle. The Romans, however, did not display the same eagerness as the Carthaginians. [3]Scipio was a new commander over raw recruits, who were, moreover, dismayed by recent portents. Hannibal saw around him a veteran army, that had marched victorious from the Pillars of Hercules. On their right and on their left the Carthaginians were shut [4]in by two seas,[5] behind[6] hung [4]over them the Alps, before[6] them the enemy: they must conquer or die. [7]If victorious, there would be an ample recompense — [8]all the accumulated fruits of Rome's many triumphs. A battle was fought, and the Romans were defeated. Scipio himself was wounded, and would have been slain,[9] if he had not been rescued[9] by the intervention of his son, who afterwards won the glory of [10]finishing the war.

[1] See Ex. XVII. N. 8. [2] Use the impers. const. [3] "Suggestions," 3. [4] What tense? A. & G. 277. a. H. 469. [5] § 16. [6] A. & G. 260. b. H. 434. I. [7] I.e. *to them victorious.* [8] "Suggestions," 10. [9] A. & G. 308. H. 510. [10] I.e. *of the war finished.* § 19.

XXI.—Chaps. 48, 52–56.

The Battle of the Trebia.

[1]Scipio, [2]finding that the open plains were not a suitable battle-field for the Romans, on account of the superiority of the Carthaginian cavalry, hastened across the Po to Placentia. [3]Occupying a strong position there, he waited until [4]his colleague arrived from Sicily. Sempronius had already sent his troops to Ariminum; thence he marched to the Trebia, where he effected[5] a junction[5] with Scipio. Hannibal was eager to force the battle while the better of the Roman generals was disabled[6] by a wound, and resolved to lure the impetuous and headstrong Sempronius to an engagement. [7]By ordering the Numidian cavalry to cross the Trebia and discharge missiles at the sentries, and then to retreat gradually, he drew the Roman army after him across the river. It was [8]towards midwinter, and the day was cold, and snow filled the air. The Romans, pursuing the retreating Numidians, had to wade breast-deep through the icy[4] stream, as the piercing sleet blew in their faces. [9]The men, numbed with cold, tired and hungry, for they had marched hurriedly out [10]without their breakfast, were obliged to face the Carthaginians, who had made their limbs supple with oil, and leisurely enjoyed their morning meal. In the battle that followed, the Romans met with a crushing defeat.

[1] §§ 22, 23. [2] § 7. [3] Abl. Abs. [4] What mood? A. & G. 328. H. 519. [5] § 1. [6] § 16. [7] Turn "He ordered the cavalry, having crossed, etc., to discharge missiles, and then by retreating, to draw." [8] brūmae tempus, or sub brumā. [9] §§ 21, 22, 23. [10] Abl. Abs.

XXII.

At daybreak came news that[1] the enemy was encamped not more[2] than ten miles off.[3] The commander-in-chief then called a halt and held a review of his troops. He likewise sent off some[4] messengers with a letter asking[5] for immediate reinforcements.[6] When these had arrived orders were given to march along the sea-shore, and in three days they came in sight of the enemy. At once the general proceeded[7] to[8] draw up his army in battle-array, as the nature of the place allowed, on the site of a plundered and half-ruined[9] city. A council of his staff-officers[10] was called, and it was decided where each one should direct[11] his operations. Afterwards he called his soldiers together and made a brief harangue. [12] "I do not think it worth while," said he in closing,[13] "to address you longer, nor to recount the glorious exploits of yourselves and your ancestors in the past; for I hold[14] it as a thing well ascertained that an army does not become energetic[15] instead of [16]slothful, or brave instead of cowardly, by the speech of its commander. I need not remind you that the senate tried every expedient to maintain the' peace that the state might be free from guilt, and that the sword was not drawn till the enemy had already invaded our territory, and committed shocking depredations without resistance." •

[1] § 1. [2] A. & G. 247. c. H. 417. N. 2. [3] If the place from which the distance is reckoned is not specified, $\bar{a}$ or ab used adverbially in the sense 'off' may accompany the ablative. H. 379. 2. N. [4] Not necessary to the sense. [5] Purpose. [6] auxilium. [7] § 4. [8] instruere āciem. [9] sēmirūtus. [10] lēgāti. [11] cūrō. A. & G. 294. d. H. 544. N. 2. [12] Employ Ind. Nar. [13] perōrāns. [14] compertum habeō. A. & G. 292. c. [15] strēnuus. [16] prō.

XXIII.

When at the beginning of 534,[1] he [2]fell by the hands
of an assassin, the Carthaginian officers of the Spanish
army summoned to fill his place Hannibal, the eldest son
of Hamilcar. He was still a young man, — born in 505,[1]
— and now, therefore, in his twenty-ninth year; but his
life[3] had already been fraught with varied experience.
While still a boy,[4] he had followed his father to the
camp; and he soon distinguished himself. His light
and firmly built[5] frame made him an excellent runner
and boxer, and a fearless rider; the [6]privation of sleep
did not affect him, and he knew like a soldier how to
enjoy or to want his food. Although his youth had
been spent in the camp, he possessed[7] such culture[8] as
was bestowed on the noble Phœnicians of his time : in
Greek, apparently after he had become a general, he
made such progress[9] under the guidance of his intimate
friend Sosilus of Sparta as to be able to compose state
papers[10] in that language. Thereafter, he had commanded the cavalry under his sister's husband, Hasdrubal, and distinguished himself by brilliant personal bravery as well as by his talents as a leader. —MOMMSEN.

[1] I.e. according to the Roman method of reckoning. *At the
beginning of the year* was variously expressed in Latin : **annō
ineunte, ïncipiente; annī initiō, principiō, exōrdiō.** [2] ob-
trunci, *assassinate;* or, **īnsīdiīs interficī.** [3] § 17. [4] A. & G.
184. H. 363. 2. 2). [5] **compāctum āc fīrmum.** [6] **vigiliae.**
[7] A. & G. 231. R. *In* with *esse,* however, must be used to denote
the possession of some quality or characteristic. [8] **cultus animī.**
[9] *to make progress in anything :* **prōficere in aliquā rē.** [10] lit-
terae pūblicae.

XXIV.

The voice of his comrades now summoned him — their
tried, although youthful general — to the chief command,
and he could now execute the designs for which his
father and his brother-in-law had lived and died. He
took possession of the inheritance,[1] and he was worthy of
it. His contemporaries [2] tried [3] to cast stains [4] of all sorts
on his character: the Romans charged him with cruelty,
the Carthaginians with covetousness; and it is true that
he hated as only Oriental natures [5] know how to hate, and
that a general who never [6] fell short of money and stores
can hardly have been [7] other than covetous. Neverthe-
less, though anger and envy and meanness have written
his history, they have not been able to mar [8] the pure and
noble image [9] which it presents. Every page of the history of the times attests his genius [10] as a general. The
power which he wielded over men is shown by his incom-
parable control over an army of various nations and many
tongues, — an army which never in the worst times muti-
nied [11] against him. He was a great man; wherever he
went he riveted the eyes of all. — MOMMSEN.

[1] *to enter on the possession of an inheritance:* hērēdĭtātem
adīre. [2] hŏmĭnēs illōrum temporum. [3] A. & G. 277. c. H. 469.
2. 1. § 4. [4] *to stain a person's reputation* is dē fāmā alĭcūĭus
dētrahere, or alĭcuī īnfāmĭam afferre. [5] § 17. [6] dēsum.
[7] alĭus atque. A. & G. 247. d. H. 459. 2. [8] dēfōrmō. [9] spĕcĭēs.
[10] "Suggestions," 9. [11] *to mutiny:* facĕre, movēre sēdĭtĭōnem.

XXV.

Scipio meanwhile held councils[1] of war in Massilia as
to the proper mode of occupying the ferries of the Rhone,
and was not induced to move even by the urgent mes-
sages that came from the leaders of the Celts. He dis-
trusted their accounts, and he [2]contented himself with
detaching a weak Roman cavalry division to reconnoitre
the left bank of the Rhone.   This detachment found the
whole enemy's army already transported to that bank,
and occupied in bringing over the elephants, which alone
remained on the right bank of the stream; and, after it
had warmly engaged some Carthaginian squadrons in the
district of Avignon[3] for the purpose of enabling it to
complete its reconnaissance, — the first encounter of the
Romans and Carthaginians in this war, — it hastily returned to report at headquarters.   Scipio now started in
utmost haste for Avignon; but when he arrived there,
even the Carthaginian cavalry that had been left behind
to cover the passage of the elephants had already taken
its departure three days ago, and nothing remained for
the consul but to return with weary troops and little
credit to Massilia, and to revile the "cowardly flight" of
the Carthaginians. — MOMMSEN.

[1] *to hold a council of war:* **cōnsilium mīlitāre habēre.**   [2] *to
be contented:* **satis habēre** (foll. by infin.).   [3] Latin: **Aveuio
(-ōnis).**

PARALLEL PASSAGES.

XXVI.

[For Parallel Passage, read Livy II. 10.]

ROMAN HEROISM: HORATIUS COCLES.

And as [1] the Etruscans approached, they took the hill Janiculum, and drove the Romans back over the wooden bridge [2] into the city. Then the Romans were seized [3] with great [4] fear; and they did not [5] venture to oppose the enemy, and to defend the entrance of the bridge, but they fled across the bridge back into the city. When Horatius, who was surnamed [6] Cocles, saw this, he placed himself opposite to the enemy at the entrance of the bridge, and two warriors, who were called Larcius and Herminius, stayed with him. These three men stirred not from the place, but fought alone with the whole army of the Etruscans, and held their position while the Romans pulled down the bridge behind them. [7] And when only a few planks were left, Larcius and Herminius hurried back, but Horatius would [8] not move until [9] the bridge was broken down and fell into the river. Then he turned round, and with his arms upon him, just as he was, sprang into the Tiber [10] and swam back to Rome unhurt. — IHNE.

[1] **cum** : A. & G. 325. H. 521. [2] Pōns Sublicius. [3] § 16. [4] H. 561. III. [5] In Latin the tendency is to combine the negative in a sentence with the connective. [6] 231. b. H. 387. N. 1. [7] Abl. Abs. [8] § 5. [9] A. & G. 328. H. 387. N. 1. [10] A. & G. 56. a. 1. H. 62. II. 2.

XXVII.

[For Parallel Passage, read Livy II. 39, 40.]

MARCH OF THE VOLSCIANS TOWARDS ROME.

(*a*) The Volscians at last advanced to Rome, and
encamping[1] near[2] the Fossa Cluilia, five miles from the
town, they laid waste the lands of the plebeians round
about. Then the Romans were seized with despair, and
scarcely retaining courage to defend the walls of the
town, did not dare to advance against the Volscians, or
fight them in the field. They looked for deliverance[3]
from the mercy and generosity[4] of their conquerors, and
sent the principal senators[5] as ambassadors to Coriolanus,
to sue for peace. But Coriolanus answered that, unless
the Romans should restore to the Volscians all the conquered towns, [6] peace could not be thought of. When the
same ambassadors came a second time,[7] to ask for more
favorable conditions, Coriolanus would not even see
them. Thereupon the chief priests appeared in their
festive robes, and with the sacred signs of their office,
and tried to calm[8] the anger of Coriolanus. But they
strove in vain. At last the noblest Roman matrons came
to Veturia, the mother of Coriolanus, and to Volumnia,
his wife, and persuaded them[9] to accompany them[9] to
the enemy's camp, and with their prayers and tears to
save the town. — IHNE.

[1] Remember that the English (but not the Latin) pres. part. is
often used loosely with *completed* sense. § 7. [2] A. & G. 153.
[3] § 1. [4] **benīgnitās**. [5] If 'as' signifies 'in the capacity of,' it is
not to be translated, and the title or function is to be placed in
apposition to the subject. [6] *to discuss terms of peace:* **agere dē
pāce**. [7] See Ex. V. N. 10. [8] **sēdāre**. [9] How distinguished in Latin?

(*b*) Now when[1] the procession[2] of Roman matrons approached the Volscian camp, and Coriolanus recognized[3] his mother, his wife, and his little children, his heart softened, and he heard the entreaties of the matrons, fell on the neck of his mother and of his beloved wife, and granted their request. He immediately led the army of the Volscians away from Rome, and gave back all the conquered towns. But he never returned to Rome, because he had been banished by the people.

As a punishment for this treachery, which the Volscians, as it appears, were obliged to submit to,[4] they were reported to have cruelly[5] murdered[6] Coriolanus at the end of the campaign.[7] Yet another, and probably older, form of the legend[8] says nothing of this revenge, but allows him to attain[9] a great age among the Volscians, and to lament his banishment from his fatherland. The simple-minded[10] old annalist saw nothing unnatural[11] in the fact that a Roman exile should restore to the Romans towns conquered by the military strength of the Volscians. — IHNE.

[1] A. & G. 324. H. 518. [2] **āgmen**: or an *impersonal construction* may be employed. §§ 1, 16. [3] **āgnōscō**: distinguish between āgnōscō and cōgnōscō. [4] **subeō.** [5] See Ex. XIV. N. 2. [6] Distinguish between **interficere, caedere, necāre, trūcidāre, iugulāre.** [7] **bellum** or **stipendium.** [8] **fābula.** [9] Distinguish between **cōnsequī** (to attain *by exertion*), **nancīscī** (*by chance*), **adipīscī** (*by good fortune*), **impetrāre** (*through asking*). [10] **crēdulus.** [11] Translate by a phrase.

XXVIII.

[*For Parallel Passage, read Livy II.* 48, 49, 50.]

The Patriotism of the Fabii.

The Veientines kept[1] Rome[2] in a continual state of alarm by constant invasions, driving away the flocks and destroying the crops.   In order to protect the community from such annoyances, the noble house of the Fabii offered to undertake the war themselves.   The consul, Kaeso Fabius, placed himself at the head of his kindred; with 306 men of patrician rank he left the town, [3]followed by the blessings and good wishes of the admiring people.   He erected a fortified camp in the territory of the Veientines, not far from the chief town of Veii, on the river Cremera.   From this spot the Fabii made the territory of the Veientines insecure,[4] and at the same time kept the enemy from attacking Rome.   But the Veientines enticed them out of their fortress into an ambush, and attacked them from all sides with overwhelming force.   Not one of the valiant band escaped. The whole race would have become extinct,[5] if[6] it had not been that one boy had been left behind in Rome, who preserved the name and the race of the Fabii. — IHNE.

[1] *kept in a constant state of alarm :* translated by one word. A. & G. 277.   H. 469. II.   [2] § 17.   [3] "Suggestions," 10.   [4] A. & G. 239. a. N. 1.   H. 373. N. 2.   [5] **exstingui.**   [6] A. & G. 315.   H. 508. 3.

XXIX.

[For Parallel Passage, read Livy III. 27, 28.]

STORY OF CINCINNATUS.

Then the Master of the People and the Master of the Horse went together into the forum, and[1] ordered[2] that every man who was of an age to go out to battle should be ready in the Field of Mars before sunset. So the army was ready at the time appointed, and they set forth from the city, [1]and made such haste, that ere the night was half[3] spent they came to Algidus; and when they perceived that they were near the enemy they made a halt.[4] Then Lucius rode on and saw how the camp of the enemy lay; and he ordered his soldiers to throw down their baggage into one place. Then they set out again in their order of march as[5] they had come from Rome, and spread themselves round the camp of the enemy on every side. When this [6]was done, upon a given signal they raised a great shout, which rang through the camp of the enemy and filled them with fear; and it sounded even to the camp of the Romans who were shut up in the valley; and the consul's men said one to another, [7]"Rescue is surely at hand, for that is the shout of the Romans." — ARNOLD.

[1] § 12. [2] A. & G. 271. b. H. 535. II. [3] A. & G. 193. H. 440. 2. N. 1. [4] § 1. [5] Render by a rel. pron. A. & G. 202. c. [6] § 201. e. H. 463. [7] Indirect Narration.

XXX.

[For Parallel Passage, read Livy V. 21.]

The Capture of Veii.

At last the day for storming the town arrived, and Camillus let[1] the Roman army advance to the walls and pretend to attack them. But while the Veientines were engaged in defending[2] the walls, a select body[3] of men advanced through the tunnel. At their head[4] was Camillus himself, and when he arrived at the place where the tunnel ended and where there was only a thin wall to break through, inside the temple of Juno, in the citadel of Veii, he heard the high priest of the Veientines, who was performing a sacrifice before the king, say[5] that whoever presented[6] this offering to the tutelar[7] goddess of Veii would be victorious in battle. [8]At this moment the Romans burst forth out of the ground; Camillus seized the victim and offered it on the altar of the goddess, and his troops dispersed themselves from the citadel over the whole town, and opened the gates to their comrades. Thus Veii fell into the hands of the Romans, and a more splendid triumphal procession than that which Camillus celebrated on his return[9] from Veii had never been seen in Rome. — Ihne.

[1] **Iubeō.** A. & G. 271. b. H. 535. II. [2] *were engaged in defending.* A. & G. 277. H. 469. II. § 4. [3] § 17. [4] § 1. [5] A. & G. 292. e. H. 535. I. 4. [6] A. & G. 316, 337. H. 507. III. 2. [7] Translate by a rel. cl. [8] § 21. [9] Best rendered perhaps by making it the subject. See ch. 23.

XXXI.

[For Parallel Passage, read Livy VI. 3.]

CAMILLUS DEFEATS THE ETRUSCANS.

The dictator now learnt that an Etruscan army, probably from Tarquinii, was besieging Sutrium. Camillus hastened[1] to its aid, but on his way, said the story of his exploits, he met the citizens of Sutrium in forlorn plight, they having been obliged to surrender their city and having saved nothing but their lives. [2] They fell on their knees before him,[3] told him their sad case,[4] and craved his assistance. He bade[5] them be of good cheer,[6] saying[7] that it was now the turn[8] of the Etruscans to wail and weep. Then he advanced upon Sutrium, and found, as he had expected,[9] that the enemy kept no watch,[10] and were thinking of nothing but plunder. He instantly forced his way into the place, made a great slaughter,[10] and a still greater number of prisoners; and Sutrium was thus, according to the story, "lost and recovered" in a day again.[11] Thus the enemies of Rome were checked,[12] and time was gained for the state to recover from its disorder and distress, and to meet its rivals on more equal terms. — ARNOLD.

[1] § 21. [2] How connected with the preceding? [3] **sē ad pedēs advolvere, provolvere; sē ad genū prōicere.** [4] Use **rēs affectae,** and join with the following verb. [5] A. & G. 331. a. H. 535. II. [6] **bonō esse animō,** or an adjective. [7] A. & G. 336. N. 2. H. 523. I. N. [8] Is best omitted in translation. [9] A. & G. 200. e. [10] "Suggestions," 10. Translate *thoughts,* not *words.* [11] § 3. [12] **supprimō.**

XXXII.

[For Parallel Passage, read Livy VIII. 6, 7.]

ROMAN DISCIPLINE: THE STORY OF MANLIUS.

When the war with the Latins had broken out, and both the hostile armies lay encamped against each other in Campania, the consuls issued orders to avoid all irregular fighting, and to take up the combat only on the explicit command of their superior officers.[1] Then it happened that the son of the consul, T. Manlius, who led a troop of cavalry, approached the enemy's camp, and was challenged[2] by Mettius, the commander of the Tusculan horse. [3]Stung by the contemptuous words of the Tusculan, the [4]fiery youth forgot the injunction of his father, accepted the challenge, and killed Mettius. In triumph he returned to the camp, decorated with the arms of his slain enemy, and accompanied by an exulting crowd of his men. With a gloomy look his father turned away from him, assembled immediately the whole army by the blast of the trumpet, and [5]pronounced the sentence of death over his victorious son. The safety[6] of the state was not to suffer from parental indulgence. In the contest of duty and paternal love, the feeling of the Roman citizen triumphed. — IHNE.

[1] Use **praefectus**, or phrase **qui praeest**, for *superior officer.*
§ 1. [2] *to challenge any one:* **aliquem ad pūgnam prōvocāre.**
[3] Consult Lat.-Eng. Dict. under **mordeō.** [4] **iuvenis ardentis animī.** [5] A. & G. 220. a. H. 410. III. N. 2. [6] § 17.

XXXIII.

[For Parallel Passages, read Livy IX. 3, 4, 5, 6, and 7.]

(a) *Roman Defeat at the Caudine Pass.*

The disasters[1] of the Caudine Forks, a defile between Campania and Samnium, [2]left a vivid impression on the national memo'ry, for it was[3] there that the legions were enclosed as in a trap and forced to an ignominious surrender. The enemies themselves, we read, startled at such unheard-of fortune, sent in haste to ask Herennius Pontius, the aged father of their general, [4]how they should act in such a crisis. His answer[5] was that they [6]should let them all go freely forth unhurt,[7] [8]and so appeal to their best and warmest feelings, or, failing that, put them all without distinction to the sword, that the loss might cripple the state for many a year. There was no safe course, he said, between the two extremes. Yet the Samnites tried to find one. They made their prisoners lay down their arms and pass under the yoke, while the officers of highest rank bound themselves as sponsors for a treaty which was to free the soil of Samnium from the arms and colonies of Rome, [9]and leave the rivals fairly balanced as before. — CAPES.

[1] **Clādēs.** *To sustain a disaster* = **clādem accipere.** Express the participle in Latin : *received at.* [2] *to retain something in the memory :* **aliquid memoriā tenēre, alicūius memoriam retinēre.** [3] § 2. [4] A. & G. 338. H. 529. [5] § 1. [6] A. & G. 294. b. H. 234. [7] A. & G. 186. b. 3. [8] I.e. *so that the enemy might be moved by so great kindness.* [9] "Suggestions," 10. §§ 3, 21.

(b) *The Romans pass under the Yoke.*

When consuls, quæstors, and tribunes of the soldiers had taken the oaths, the first fulfilment[1] of the treaty followed. The Romans gave up their arms, and marched out of the camp, wearing[2] or carrying with them nothing but one single article of clothing, the campestre or kilt, reaching from the waist[3] to the knees, [4]and leaving the upper part of the body naked, now that the soldiers had been obliged to give up their[5] coats of mail. The six hundred knights were then delivered up to the Samnites, and the rest of the Roman army, stripped[6] of their arms and baggage, passed in order through an opening purposely made for them in the Samnite lines of blockade. Two spears were set upright in this opening, and a third was fastened across them at the top; and through this gateway the vanquished army marched out, as a token that they had been conquered in war, and owed their lives to the enemy's mercy. It was no peculiar insult devised for this occasion, but a common usage, so far as appears, in all similar cases : like the modern ceremony[7] of piling arms[8] when a garrison or army surrender themselves as [9]prisoners of war. — ARNOLD.

[1] § 1. [2] § 7. See also A. & G. 247. d. H. 459. 2. [3] **media pars corporis.** [4] I.e. *so that.* §§ 3, 21. [5] **lōrīca.** [6] **exuō.** For construction, see A. & G. 225. d. H. 384. II. 2. [7] "Suggestions," 9. [8] *to pile arms:* **arma in ūnum locum cōnferre.** [9] See Ex. XXVII. N. 5.

(c) *The Army returns to Rome.*

In far different plight,[1] and with far other feelings, than they had entered the pass of Caudium, did the Roman army issue out from it again upon the plain of Campania. Defeated and disarmed, they knew not what reception[2] they might meet with from their Campanian allies. But the Campanians behaved faithfully and generously: they sent supplies[3] of arms, of clothing, and of provisions to meet the Romans even before they arrived at Capua; and when the army approached[4] their city, the senate and people went out to meet them. No attentions,[5] however, could[6] soothe[7] the wounded pride of the Romans: they could not bear to raise their eyes from the ground nor to speak to any one: full of shame, they continued[8] their march to Rome. When they came near to it, all those soldiers who had a home in the country dispersed and escaped to their several houses singly and silently; whilst those who lived in Rome lingered without the walls till the sun was set, and stole to their homes[9] under cover of the darkness. — ARNOLD.

[1] **Fortūna.** [2] Use the verb **excipiō.** [3] Unnecessary in translation. [4] Employ dative of the part. with **obviam ēgredior.** A. & G. 228. b. [5] **comitās.** [6] § 5. [7] **dēleniō.** [8] § 4. [9] **per noctem.**

(d) *Humiliation of the People.*

[1]Nor was the blow less deeply felt by the senate and by the whole people. The actual[2] loss in the battle, and the captivity[3] of six hundred of the youth of Rome, were enough of themselves to throw the nation into mourning; how much more grievous were they when accompanied by such utter defeat and humiliation. All business was suspended; all orders put on mourning; the knights and senators laid aside their gold rings, and took off the well-known red border of their dress which marked their rank[4]; in every house there was weeping and wailing for those who had returned home dishonored,[5] no less than for those who were dead and captive; and all ceremonies of rejoicing, all festivals, and all private marriages were suspended, till they could be celebrated in a year of better omen. A dictator was named to hold the comitia for the election of the new consuls; but the augurs declared that the appointment was null and void; another dictator was then chosen, but the same objection was repeated, till at last, as if the gods abhorred every magistrate of this fatal year, the elections were held by an interrex. — ARNOLD.

[1] § 17.   [2] **ipse.**   [3] § 17.   [4] "Suggestions," 10.   [5] **ignominiae plēnī.**

XXXIV.

[For Parallel Passage, read Livy X. 27, 28.]

ROMAN DEVOTION TO THE STATE: P. DECIUS.

When the armies closed, the Roman left wing struggled[1] vigorously against the numbers, and strength[2], and courage of the Gauls. Twice, it is said[3], did the Roman and Campanian cavalry charge with effect the Gaulish horsemen; but they were at length driven back upon their infantry. The first line of the legions was broken, and the Gauls, following their advantage, pressed on with the masses of their infantry. Decius strove in vain to stop the flight of his soldiers. One way alone was left by which he might yet serve his country: he bethought[4] him of his father at the battle of Vesuvius, and calling to M. Livius, one of the pontifices who attended him in the field, he desired him to dictate to him the fit words for self-devotion.[5] Then, in the same dress, and with all the same ceremonies, he pronounced also the same form of words which had been uttered by his father, and devoting himself and the host of the enemy with him to the grave and to the powers of the dead, he · rode into the midst of the Gaulish ranks, and was slain. — ARNOLD.

[1] Use the impers. const. with **pūgnō**. [2] See Ex. I. N. 6. [3] A. & G. 330. a. and b. H. 534. 1. [4] A. & G. 219. H. 406. II. [5] § 1.

XXXV.

[For Parallel Passage, read Livy XXII. 2.]

The passage of the Apennines was accomplished without much difficulty, at a point as far west as possible, or,
in other words, as distant as possible[1] from the enemy;
but the marshy lowlands between the Serchio[2] and the
Arno were so flooded by the melting of the snow and
the spring rains, that the army had to march four days
in water, [3] without finding any other dry spot for resting
by night than was supplied by piling the baggage, or
by the sumpter animals[4] that had fallen. The troops
underwent unutterable sufferings, particularly the Gallic
infantry, which marched behind the Carthaginians along
tracks[5] already rendered impassable: they murmured
loudly, and would undoubtedly have dispersed to a man,[6]
had not the Carthaginian cavalry under Mago, which
brought up the rear, rendered flight impossible. Various
diseases decimated[7] the soldiers; Hannibal himself [8]lost
an eye in consequence of ophthalmia.[9] — MOMMSEN.

---

[1] A. & G. 93. H. 170. 2.   [2] Latin name, **Auser (-eris)**.   [3] See
Ex. X. N. 9.   [4] **iūmentum (sarcinārium)**.   [5] 258. g.   H. 420.
1. 3).   [6] **omnēs ad ūnum**.   [7] **decimō** is late Latin, and should be
avoided. "Suggestions," 9.   [8] *to lose one eye :* **alterō oculō capī**.
Consult Lat.-Eng. Dict. under **capiō**.   [9] **oculōrum īnflammātio**.

XXXVI.

[For Parallel Passage, read Livy XXIV. 7 and 21.]

ASSASSINATION OF HIERONYMUS, KING OF SYRACUSE.

An empty house [1] in this street had been occupied by the conspirators: when the king came opposite to it, one of their number,[2] who was one of the king's guards, and close to his person, stopped just behind him, as if something had caught his foot; and whilst he seemed trying to get free, he checked the advance [3] of the following multitude, and [4] left the king to go on a few steps unattended. [4] At that moment the conspirators rushed out of the house and murdered him. So sudden was the act,[5] that his guards could not save him; seeing [6] him dead,[7] they were seized with a panic and dispersed. The murderers [8] hastened, some into the market-place of Leontini, to raise the cry [5] of liberty there, and others to Syracuse, to anticipate the king's friends and secure the city for themselves and the Romans. Their tidings, however, had flown [9] before them; and Andranodorus, the king's uncle, had already secured the island of Ortygia,[10] in which was the citadel. The assassins arrived just at nightfall,[11] calling the people to rise in the name of liberty. — ARNOLD.

[1] § 16. H. 561. [2] § 17. [3] Contained in the verbal idea. § 1. [4] What is the relation between the two sentences? §§ 3, 21. What word may be omitted in the translation? [5] § 1. [6] The pres. part. is used more freely in English than in Latin. How may it be rendered here? [7] A. & G. 186. c. [8] For the use of a distributive apposition, see Madvig, § 217. Obs. 1. [9] "Suggestions," 10. [10] A. & G. 183. H. 363. [11] **sub noctem.**

XXXVII.

[For Parallel Passage, read Livy XXIV. 34.]

SIEGE OF SYRACUSE.

Marcellus brought up his ships against the sea[1]-wall of Achradina, and endeavored by a constant discharge[2] of stones and arrows to clear the walls of their defenders, so that his men might apply their ladders, and mount to the assault.[3] These ladders rested on two ships, lashed together [4]broadside to broadside, [5]and worked as one by their outside oars. But Archimedes had supplied the ramparts with an artillery [6]so powerful that it overwhelmed the Romans before they could get[7] within the range[8] which their missiles could reach; and when they came closer, they found[9] that all the lower part of the wall was loopholed; and their men were struck down[10] with fatal aim by an enemy they could not see. At other times machines like cranes were thrust out over the wall; and the end of the lever with an iron grapple affixed to it was lowered upon the ships. [11]As soon as the grapple had taken hold, the other end of the lever was lowered by heavy weights, and the ship raised out of the water, till it was made almost to stand upon its stern; then the grapple was suddenly let go,[12] and the ship[13] dropped into the sea with a violence which either upset it or filled it with water. — ARNOLD.

[1] Express by a rel. cl. [2] § 19. [3] § 1. [4] Express by a result cl. [5] § 21. [6] **tormenta.** [7] A. & G. 262, 327. H. 520. [8] *to come within reach of a missile* is **intrā tēlī coniectum venīre.** [9] § 3. [10] § 16. [11] A. & G. 346. a–c. H. 573. §§ 22–24. [12] § 21. [13] Avoid a change of subject.

XXXVIII.

[For Parallel Passage, read Livy XXVII. 39.]

HASDRUBAL'S MARCH INTO ITALY.

As soon as the winter snows were thawed,[1] Hasdrubal commenced his march from Auvergne[2] to the Alps. [3] He experienced none of the difficulties which his brother had met with from the mountain tribes. The fame of the war, with which Italy had now been convulsed[4] for twelve years, had penetrated into the Alpine passes, and the mountaineers now understood that a mighty city southward of the Alps was to be attacked[5] by the troops whom they saw marching among them. They now not only opposed no resistance to the passage of Hasdrubal, but many of them, out of the love of enterprise and plunder, or allured by the high pay he offered, took service with him; and thus he advanced upon Italy with an army that gathered strength at every league. Many warriors of the Ligurian tribes joined him; and crossing the river Po, he marched down its southern bank to the city of Placentia, which he wished to secure [6] as a base for his future operations.[7] Placentia resisted him as bravely as it had resisted Hannibal twelve years before, and for some time Hasdrubal was occupied with a fruitless siege before its walls. — CREASY.

[1] dilābor: see Livy XXI. 36. [2] Avernī. [3] "Suggestions," 10. [4] concutiō. [5] A. & G. 147. c; 288. f; 302. R. H. 537. [6] Turn *'that thence he might conduct military operations.'* [7] "Suggestions," 10.

XXXIX.

[For Parallel Passage, read Livy XXVII. 44.]

BEFORE THE BATTLE OF METAURUS.

Meanwhile at Rome the [1]news of Nero's expedition had caused the greatest excitement and alarm. All men felt [2] the full audacity [3] of the enterprise,[4] but hesitated [2] what epithet [5] to apply to it. It was evident that Nero's conduct [6] would be judged of by the event, that most unfair criterion,[4] as the Roman historian truly terms it. People reasoned [7] on the perilous state in which Nero had left the rest [8] of the army, without a general and deprived of the core [9] of its strength, in the vicinity of the terrible Hannibal. [10] All these calamities had come to them while they had only one Carthaginian general and army to deal with in Italy. Now they had two Punic wars at a time. They had two Carthaginian armies; they had almost two Hannibals in Italy. Hasdrubal was sprung from the same father; [11] trained up in the same hostility to Rome; equally practised in battle against their legions; and if the comparative speed and success with which he had crossed the Alps was a fair test, he was even a better general than his brother. — CREASY.

[1] Render by a verbal clause. [2] What tense? [3] § 17. [4] § 1. [5] "Suggestions," 10. [6] § 17. [7] May be entirely omitted. What construction follows? [8] A. & G. 193. H. 440. N. 1. [9] "Suggestions," 10. [10] Employ Indirect Narration. A. & G. 336. 2. N. 2. [11] A. & G. 244. a. H. 415. II.

XL.

[For Parallel Passage, read Livy XXVII. 47-49.]

BATTLE OF METAURUS.

Nero found Marcus Livius at Lena Gallica awaiting[1] the enemy; both consuls at once marched against Hasdrubal, whom they found occupied in crossing the Metaurus. Hasdrubal wished to avoid a battle and to escape from the Romans by a detour,[2] but his guides abandoned[3] him; he[3] lost his way on ground that was strange to him, and was at length attacked on the march[4] by the Roman cavalry, and detained until[5] the Roman infantry arrived, and a battle became inevitable.[6] Hasdrubal stationed the Spaniards on the right wing, with his ten elephants in front of it, and the Gauls on the left, which he held back. Long the fortune of battle wavered on the right wing, and the consul Livius who commanded there was hard pressed, till Nero,[7] repeating as a tactical manœuvre the strategical operation which had succeeded so well, allowed the enemy opposite to him to remain as they stood, and marching round his own army, fell upon the flank of the Spaniards. This decided the day. The severely bought and very bloody victory was complete. Hasdrubal, when he saw the admirably conducted battle was lost, sought and found, like his father, an honorable soldier's death. — MOMMSEN.

[1] **exspectō.** [2] Consult Dict. under **circumdō.** [3] Distinguish between **deserere, relinquere, dēstituere.** Distinguish between **errāre vagāre, pālāri.** Cf. Doederlein, Synon. 1. 89: errāmus incertī, vagāmur solūtī, pālāmur dispersī. [4] **in itinere.** [5] A. & G. 328. H. 519. [6] Express by a circumlocution: **vītārī nōn posse.** [7] "Suggestions," 10.

XLI.

[For Parallel Passage, read Livy XXVII. 50.]

AFTER THE BATTLE.

From the moment[1] that Nero's march had been heard
of at Rome, intense anxiety possessed the whole city.
Every day the senate sat from sunrise to sunset; and
not[2] a senator was absent; every day the forum was
crowded from morning till evening, as each hour might
bring some great tidings, and every man wished to be
[3]among the first to hear them. A doubtful rumor arose
that a great battle [4]had been fought, and a great victory
won only two days before: two horsemen of Narnia had
ridden off from the field to carry the news to their home.
But men dared not lightly believe what they so much
wished to be true; and how, they said, could a battle
fought in the extremity [5]of Umbria be heard of only
two days after at Rome? Soon, however, it was known
that a letter had arrived from L. Manlius Acidinus himself, who commanded the army at Narnia: the horsemen had certainly arrived there from the field of battle,
and brought tidings[4] of a glorious victory. The letter
was read first in the senate and then in the forum from
the rostra. — ARNOLD.

[1] I.e. *from what time.* [2] A. & G. 209. b. II. 569. IV. 1. See
Ex. XXVI. 5. [3] § 2. [4] § 1. [5] A. & G. 193. H. 440. N. 1.

XLII.

[Before doing this exercise, read Livy IX. 13–16.]

L. Papirius Cursor was one of the favorite heroes of
Roman tradition; his remarkable swiftness of foot, his
gigantic strength, and the iron strictness of his discipline, accompanied as it was by occasional touches of
rough humor, all contributed to make his memory popu-
lar, somewhat in the same way as Richard Cœur de Lion
has been admired among us; and his countrymen boasted
that he would have been a worthy champion to have
fought against Alexander the Great, if Alexander had
ever invaded Italy. This favorite leader was consul
in the year immediately following the affair of the pass
of Caudium; so great a warrior must have signally
avenged that disgrace; and accordingly he was made
to realize the most sanguine wishes of the national
vanity; he retook Luceria, the fatal town which had
tempted the consuls of the last year to rush blindly into
the defile of Caudium; and in it he recovered all the
arms and all the standards which had been taken from
the Romans, and above all he there found the six hundred Roman knights who had been given up as hostages,
and delivered them all safe and sound. — ARNOLD.

XLIII.

[Before doing this exercise, read Livy XXII. 51, 54, 55.]

EVENTS AFTER THE BATTLE OF CANNÆ.

The awful news flew to Rome. Consternation and despair seized the people. The city would have been emptied of its population, had not the senate ordered the gates to be closed. Never did that body display greater calmness, wisdom, prudence, and resolution. By word and act they bade the people never despair of the republic. Little by little the panic was allayed. Measures were concerted for the defence of the capital, as it was expected that Hannibal would immediately march to Rome. Messengers were sent along the southern military road to see, as Livy pathetically expressed it, "if the gods, touched by one pang of 'pity, had left aught remaining to the Roman name," and to bring the first tidings of the expected advance of Hannibal. The leader of the Numidian cavalry, Maharbal, urged Hannibal to follow up closely his victory. "Let me advance with the cavalry," said he, "and in five days you shall dine in the capital." But Hannibal refused to adopt the counsel of his impetuous general. Maharbal turned away, and with mingled reproach and impatience, exclaimed, "Alas! thou knowest how to gain a victory, but not how to use one." — MYERS.

XLIV.

[Before attempting this exercise, carefully study Appendix, §§ 21–24.]

The commander of the enemy's forces was an experienced general and a skilful tactician.[1] Yet when he heard of the unexpected approach of the army that had been despatched by the senate against him, and when he saw that in addition to [2] other disadvantages he had been engaged in a spot ill adapted[3] for fighting, he tried to take refuge in flight; but it was too late.[4] Throughout the camp great indignation reigned,[5] and the men hardly refrained from offering violence to the leader,[6] "by whose rashness," they said, "they had been brought into such a situation." While thus paralyzed[7] and before they could recover, their foes were upon them. Cut to pieces[8] on every side, they abandoned the contest; and disarmed, they were sent home in disgrace.

Yet the struggle had been fiercer than one might have expected from the number engaged. One who was an eyewitness[9] of this ignominious disaster,[9] and an unprejudiced[10] observer, has eloquently described the instances of bravery displayed, how the army was crushed by the overpowering[11] numbers of the enemy, and finally, when forced to surrender, the utter humiliation of a brave and spirited race.

[1] rei mīlitāris perītus. [2] praeter. [3] inīquus ad. [4] Incorporate with preceding clause. [5] "Suggestions," 10. [6] A. & G. 341. [7] See Lat.-Eng. Dict. under obstupefaciō. Cf. stupeō. [8] caedō. [9] spectātor et testes. § 13. [10] § 20. [11] "Suggestions," 10.

XLV.

[*In connection with this exercise, study carefully Appendix*, §§ 21-24.]

To such a degree does Fortune blind a people, when she is determined upon their ruin, that when danger of the greatest magnitude threatened that state which in former times had left no means untried to procure aid, and had on many occasions nominated a dictator, now when an enemy whom they had never met, or even heard of, was advancing in arms against them, looked not for any extraordinary aid or assistance. Tribunes whose rashness had brought on the troubles were entrusted with the chief command. They extenuated the importance which report gave to the war; and the consequence was that they used no greater diligence in levying forces than was usual in case of wars in their midst. Meanwhile the enemy, hearing that the violators of mankind had been rewarded with honors, and that their embassy had been insulted, were inflamed with anger, a passion which that race knows not how to control, and instantly they snatched up their ensigns and began the march in all haste. Their precipitate movement caused such alarm wherever they passed that the inhabitants of the cities ran together to arms, and the peasants betook themselves to flight; then they signified to them by loud shouts that to Rome they were going.

XLVI.

[In connection with this exercise, study Appendix, §§ 21–24.]

Soon the numerous tribes of the enemy reached the city. There the military tribunes had formed no camp, nor had taken any precaution of raising a rampart which might serve as a retreat. Regardless of their duty to gods and men, without taking auspices or offering a sacrifice, they drew up their line, which they extended on towards the wings, that they might not be surrounded by the numerous forces of the enemy. On the right was a small eminence, which they resolved to occupy with a body of reserves; and this measure, as it gave the first cause to their dismay, so it proved the only means of safety in their flight. The chieftain of the invaders thought that, as his enemies were few, he should especially be on guard against their skill. Supposing, therefore, that the higher place had been seized with this design, that when his forces should be engaged in front with the line of the legions, that reserved force might attack their rear and flank, he turned his force against that body; for he did not doubt that if he could dislodge them from their post, his troops, so much superior in number, would find an easy victory in the plain.

XLVII.

[In connection with this exercise, study Appendix, §§ 21-24.]

In the opposing army there appeared nothing like Romans, either among the commanders or soldiers. Terror and dismay had taken possession of their minds, and such a total unconcern of their duty, that by far the greater number took refuge in flight. For some time the situation of the ground defended the reserve; but those who formed the rest of the time on the flank and on their rear, no sooner heard the shout, than not only without attempting to fight, but without even returning the shout, fresh and unhurt, they ran away from an untried enemy almost before they had seen them. Thus no lives of the combatants were lost; but their rear was cut to pieces, while they crowded on one another and impeded their flight.

On the other hand, such a miraculous and speedy victory astonished the enemy. At first they stood motionless, struck with fear, as if ignorant of what had happened; then they dreaded some stratagem; finally they collected the spoils of the slain, and piled the arms in heaps, according to their practice.

XLVIII.

[In connection with this exercise, study Appendix, §§ 21-24.]

Immediately after the retreat of the Gauls all the old enemies of Rome were again in arms, in order to take advantage of the helpless condition of the Romans, and the threatened revolt of the Latins made these attacks especially dangerous. But the tried hero, Camillus, who now for the second time commanded the Roman legions as dictator, first attacked and overcame the Volscians, and reduced them to final submission after they had carried on war with Rome for seventy years. He then vanquished the Æquians, and turned with the rapidity of lightning against the Etruscans, who, with united powers, were besieging the town of Sutrium. Unable to resist any longer, the inhabitants of Sutrium had already surrendered their town, in consideration of a free retreat, and the train of poor homeless creatures, with their wailing wives and children, met Camillus, who was hastening to their relief. He immediately pushed forward to the town, where he surprised the Etruscans, as they were engaged in plundering the town, and having regained the place, restored it to the inhabitants on the same day on which they had lost it. A well-deserved triumph crowned this three-fold victory.

APPENDIX.

SUGGESTIONS

1. Never attempt to translate the English exercises into Latin without a *thorough* study of the chapters upon which they are based.

2. Cultivate a habit of close observation in reading the Latin, noticing carefully every word and phrase, every construction, and the order of words in a sentence.

3. Observe with care also the logical relation of words and clauses, which the Latin marks with greater precision than the English. Notice that the word which most clearly shows its connection with what precedes is put at the beginning of the sentence.

4. *Try to think in Latin.* Read aloud the Latin text to yourself, without translating, and try to comprehend its meaning in the Roman order.

5. Before attempting to translate the English passage into Latin, read it over carefully and endeavor to realize its meaning, and to get the thought clearly before you.

6. Read the English aloud, and note the emphatic words or phrases. Emphasis in Latin is occasionally expressed by particles, but most often by the order of the words.

7. Do the whole written exercise before referring to the Latin text upon which it is based. If it seems difficult, open your Livy to the text, read and try to understand it thoroughly,

55

then close the book, and do the best you can before you again refer to the original. Then compare and observe where the original differs from your own, and endeavor to see exactly the reasons for its superiority.

8. *Do not use an English-Latin dictionary.* In the text upon which the English passage is based will be found all the materials for the translation of that piece. ' No vice of composition is more common than the mechanical rendering of printed English *by means of a dictionary or phrase-book* into Latin writing.'

On the other hand, a good Latin-English dictionary must be freely used, especially where the student is in doubt as to the appropriateness of the word he has in mind.

9. Remember that a large number of English words come to us through the late Latin, which differs widely oftentimes from the classical language; and you must beware of using Latin words which *seem* to be the same as the English ones.

10. Before translating, reduce the English to its simplest form, stripping it of needless synonyms, and eliminating all inexactness and indistinctness. Translation from English into Latin is largely a *simplification*. The English is a richer language, and is more varied in its expression: the Latin is a simple and very direct language. The Roman fondness for simplicity is seen in the use of (a) **rēs**, 'a blank cheque, to be filled up from the context to the requisite amount of meaning'[1]; (b) **esse**, which is often to be translated by a more expressive word, *e.g.* **per castra indīgnātiō ingēns erat**, *great indignation* reigned *throughout the camp* ; (c) **hominēs**, which would translate ' men,' 'persons,' ' individuals,' 'personalities,' 'peoples,' ' the world,' ' humanity.'

---

[1] POTTS, Latin Prose Composition. The following meanings are quoted from Livy : rēs Rōmāna (*state*), ut tum rēs erant (*circumstances*), haud displicet rēs Tullō (*proposal*), rēs ad Camillum rediit (*government*), rēs nova (*novelty*), rēs novae (*revolution*), rēs secundae (*prosperity*), rēs adversae (*adversity*), tua rēs agitur (*interest*).

NOTES ON IDIOMS.

§ 1. Substantives are less often used in Latin, and must sometimes in translation be replaced by an adjective, adverb, relative or other verbal clause.

§ 2. Auxiliary verbs will be often suppressed in translation, in such expressions as, 'He was the first to do it,' 'It is you I ask' (**prīmus haec fēcit, tē rogō**) : position in Latin ofttimes giving the effect of our auxiliary verbs.

§ 3. Many other verbs, such as 'keep,' 'cease,' 'begin,' 'attempt,' 'try,' etc., disappear altogether in translation, or their force is expressed by adverbs.

§ 4. The Latin Imperfect often expresses such ideas, as 'continued to,' 'used to,' 'tried to,' 'proceeded to,' 'began to.'

§ 5. 'Would,' 'could,' etc., used as auxiliaries in subjunctive clauses, and the same words used as imperfects of 'will,' 'can,' etc., ought to be distinguished in translation. The last sense is expressed by **possum**, and certain impersonals like **licet**, etc. 'Would' is often used in a frequentative sense, and is then translated by the imperfect tense.

§ 6. Notice the difference between the Latin and English idioms with verbs of *necessity* and *possibility* ('might,' 'ought,' 'could,' etc., with infinitive). **potuī (poteram) vidēre**, *I might have seen.* **dēbuī (dēbēbam) vidēre**, *I ought to have seen.* **hōc dīxisse potest**, *he may have said this.*

The difference of idiom arises from the English defective verbs *may, ought*, etc., and the correct use of the tense in Latin may be shown by a more literal translation : *e.g.* **potuī vidēre**, *I was able to see ;* **dēbuī vidēre**, *I was bound (it was my duty) to see ;* **hōc dīxisse potest**, *it is possible that he said this.*

§ 7. The Latin Present Participle is strictly *present*, and denotes *uncompleted action contemporaneous* with that of the main verb. The English present participle is often used vaguely, and must be translated by the past participle **cum** with the subjunctive, etc.

§ 8. The Ablative Absolute may be equivalent to an adverbial clause of time, manner, condition, cause, or concession. But this construction is to be avoided, (*a*) when it stands for a subordinate clause, in which the subject denotes the same person or thing as the subject or object of the principal clause: *e.g.* **haec legēns tē vīdī** (not **mē legente**); (*b*) when the Ablative has a noun, adjective, or participle in the predicate in agreement with it: *e.g.* **cum Cicerō cōnsul creātus esset,** *when Cicero was elected Consul.*

§ 9. The Adjective in Latin often stands instead of the objective or subjective genitive, or instead of a preposition and its case, especially to denote *origin, designation of place and time, and material: e.g.* **domus rēgia,** *the palace of the king.* **Miltiadēs Athēniēnsis,** *Miltiades of Athens.* **pūgna Cannēnsis,** *the battle of Cannæ.* **iter Brundisīnum,** *the way towards Brundisium.*

Conversely, sometimes in Latin, the genitive of a noun must be used, where in English an adjective is employed: *e.g.* **hostium castra,** *hostile camps.* **omnium gaudium,** *general joy.*

§ 10. An Adjective of praise or blame is not combined with a proper name, except as a *cognomen* or *title;* but first the proper name is mentioned, and then the class with the attribute: *e.g.* **Cātō, homo doctissimus,** *the learned Cato.* **Alexander Māgnus,** *Alexander the Great.*

§ 11. If several adjectives be joined to a noun, as a rule they are connected by copulative conjunctions. Note especially the following expressions :—

> **multa et māgna incommoda,** *many great disadvantages.*
>
> **multī et optimī hominēs** ⎱
> **multī optimīque hominēs** ⎰ *many excellent men.*
> **multī, iīque optimī** ⎰

§ 12. In an enumeration of three or more co-ordinate words, either (1) each is connected with the preceding by a conjunction (polysyndeton), or (2) no conjunction is put (asyndeton): *e.g.* summā fide et cōnstantiā, et iūstitiā; or, summā fide, cōnstantiā, iūstitiā.

So aliī, cēterā, reliquī stand at the end of an enumeration, without a conjunction: *e.g.* honōrēs, dīvitiae, cētera; likewise, postrēmō, denique, and not, et postrēmō, etc.

Asyndeton occurs in quick or animated discussion: vēnī, vīdī, vīcī.

§ 13. Sometimes the Romans joined two nouns by a conjunction, where the English employs a noun with the genitive or an adjective: *e.g.* ratiō et doctrīna, *theoretical knowledge.*

This figure is called *Hendiadys.*

§ 14. The frequent use of the Relative as a connective where the English employs a personal or demonstrative pronoun ought to be carefully remembered.

§ 15. Latin was pre-eminently a language of orators and rhetoricians, and has, therefore, assumed a rhetorical color. This is seen in the frequent use of the superlative of the adjective where the English would have the positive.

§ 16. The Latin, being a very direct language in its expression, naturally prefers the Active to the Passive voice, so that the English passive is more often to be translated by the active in Latin.

But the Impersonal Passive is frequently employed where the expression is indefinite: *e.g.* hūc concurritur, *they rush for this point, a general rush is made for this point.*

§ 17. "Latin is concrete in its expression. It deals with the concrete and individual, not with the abstract and universal." Thus 'Rome' or 'Carthage' should be rendered in Latin by Rōmānī or Carthaginiēnsēs, when a quality or action of the inhabitants is spoken of.

§ 18. Verbal abstracts, as 'knowledge,' are sometimes to be rendered by the Infinitive, or, in the oblique cases, by the

Gerund: *e.g.* **grătiam dēbēre,** *the feeling of gratitude;* **fēlīcem esse,** *success;* **ad perfruendās voluptātēs,** *for the enjoyment of pleasures.*

§ 19. The Participle in agreement with a noun is sometimes used for the corresponding verbal noun with the genitive: this form is particularly employed where the verbal noun is not in good use: *e.g.* **urbs capta,** *the capture of the city;* **hae litterae recitătae,** *the reading of the letter.*

§ 20. Remember that the English sometimes expresses single ideas by double terms: *e.g.* ' feeling of shame ' (**pudor**), ' love of glory ' (**glōria**); and conversely, an English word may unite several ideas: *e.g.* 'prejudices' (**opīniōnēs praeiūdicătae,** or **falsae atque inveterăta opīniōnēs**), 'character' (**ingenium et mōrēs**), ' method' (**via et ratiō**).

THE PERIODIC STYLE IN LIVY.

§ 21. Livy and Cicero in the main adopted the periodic style, for which the Latin language, in its freedom of arrangement of words and clauses, has special aptitude. In the imitation of Livy's style, it is therefore important to understand clearly the nature of the formation of well-proportioned and rhythmical periods; and it is intended to make a short study of that style here, and to give rules which may be consulted, especially before the translation of the last seven exercises.

The student should carefully note the difference between the English and Latin style. English is essentially a language of separate or detached sentences, making clauses logically subordinate and dependent, co-ordinate and independent sentences. The Latin, on the other hand, attends more carefully to the logical relation of clauses. In the treatment of a subject it seizes upon the central idea, expresses it by a leading clause, and groups around it, by means of subordinate clauses, all accessory ideas, so as to form a symmetrical whole.

§ 22. A Period[1] is a complex sentence, in which one or more subordinate clauses are incorporated into the main clause : *e.g.* —

Scipiō, ut Hannibalem ex Ītaliā dēdūceret, exercitum in Africam trāiēcit. [Cf. Scipiō exercitum in Africam trāiecit, ut Hannibalem ex Ītaliā dēdūceret (not periodic).]

Flaminius, cum prīdiē sōlis occasū ad lacum pervēnisset, inexplōrātō posterō diē vixdum satis certā lūce angustiīs superātīs, postquam in patentiōrem campum pandī āgmen coepit, id tantum hostium, quod ex adversō erat, cōnspexit. (Livy xxii. 4.)

Numitor inter prīmum tumultum hostēs invāsisse urbem atque adortōs rēgiam dictitāns, cum pubem Albānum in arcem praesidiō armīsque obtinendam avocāsset, postquam iuvenēs perpetrātā caede pergere ad sē grātulantēs vīdit, exemplō advocātō conciliō, scelera in sē frātrēs, originem, neptōtum, ut genitī, ut ēdūcātī, ut cōgnitī essent, caedem deinde tyrannī sēque ēius auctōrem ōstendit. (Livy i. 6.)

§ 23. By a study of the above examples we observe —

(*a*) That the sense is expressed by the sentence *as a whole*, the thought and grammatical structure being not completed till the last word.

(*b*) That the main idea or leading statement is expressed by the principal sentence.

(*c*) That the circumstances of the main action are put in subordinate clauses, which are incorporated within the principal sentence, and are arranged in their natural order, *i.e.* in the order in which they naturally occur to the mind.

(*d*) That a period opens with a leading element, common to the principal and subordinate clauses, which is usually the *subject*, and is followed immediately by the subordinate clauses.

[1] From Gr. περίοδος (= circuitūs or ambitūs verbōrum). "A Period is so-called because the reader, in order to collect together the words of the principal sentence, must make a circuit, so to say, round the interpolated clauses." — POTTS, *Hints towards Latin Prose Composition*.

Hence the arrangement of the parts of a period is, in the main, as follows : —

1. The subject, with the phrases or clauses immediately con-nected with it. 2. The phrases or clauses expressing circum-stances of time, place, cause, means, etc. 3. Clauses expressing the remoter object. 4. The object, with the clauses immedi-ately connected with it. 5. The principal verb.

(e) That the subordinate ideas of a Latin period would, in English, be detailed in a number of co-ordinate and indepen-dent sentences. This may be seen in a translation of the fore-going passages from Livy : —

" Flaminius had reached the lake at sunset the day before. On the morrow, without reconnoitring and while the light was still uncertain, he traversed the narrow pass. As his army began to deploy into the widening plain, he could see only that part of the enemy's force which was in front of him." (Livy xvii. 4.)

" In the beginning of the tumult, Numitor called out that the city was assaulted by an enemy, and the palace attacked. He had drawn away the Alban youth to the citadel, on pre-tence of securing it by an armed garrison ; and in a little time, seeing the young men, after perpetrating the murder, coming towards him, with expressions of joy, he instantly called the people to an assembly, laid before them the iniquitous behavior of his brother towards himself ; the birth of his grandchildren, how they were begotten, how educated, how discovered ; then informed them of the death of the usurper, and that he had himself encouraged the design." (Livy i. 6.)

§ **24.**   SPECIAL SUGGESTIONS.

1. The element common to both principal and subordinate sentences is placed at the beginning. This, as has been stated, is commonly the *subject* of principal and subordinate sentences ; but it may also be —

(*a*) The *object*: *e.g.* —

Alcibiadem ut barbarī incendium effūgisse vīdērunt, tēlīs ēminus mīssīs interfēcērunt.

(*b*) The *object* of principal sentence, and *subject* of subordinate sentence : *e.g.* —

Scipiōnem Hannibal eō ipsō, quod adversus ēum dux esset potissimum lectus, praestantem virum crēdēbat.

(*c*) The *subject* of principal sentence, and *object* of subordinate clause : *e.g* —

Rēx Prūsias, cum Hannibalī apud eum exsulantī dēpūgnāre placēret, negābat sē audēre, quod exta prohibērent.

But usually (*b*) and (*c*) are avoided, for the same noun, as far as possible, is kept in the *same case* throughout the period.

2. Result and Final Clauses generally stand *after* the word on which they depend : *e.g.* —

Tantus repente clāmor est sublātus, ut Placentiae quoque audirētur.

3. Noun clauses, in long periods, in indirect narration, follow the principal verb : *e.g.* —

Respondit, trānsisse Rhēnum sēsē nōn suā sponte, sed rogātum et arcessītum ā Gallīs.

4. Avoid the accumulation of verbs at the end of a period : *e.g.*

Pyrrhus igitur, cum putāret sibi glōriōsum fore pācem et foedus cum Rōmānīs post victōriam facere, Rōmam mīsit lēgātum Cineam, quī pācem aequīs conditiōnibus prōpōneret.

5. For the sake of clearness, nothing extraneous to the main thought should be introduced within the period. Such accessory sentences, therefore, become parenthetical : *e.g.* —

Bellī Fidenatis contagiōne irritātī Veientium animī, et cōnsanguinitāte (nam Fīdēnātes quoque Etrūscī fuērunt) et quod ipsa loca propinquitās locī, sī Rōmāna arma omnibus īnfesta fīnitimīs essent, stimulābant.

§ 25. The following Periods from Livy may serve to illustrate these remarks and suggest special points : —

(a) Dum haec in Ītaliā geruntur, Cn. Cornēlius Scīpiō in Hispāniam cum clāsse et exercitū missus, cum ab ōstiō Rhodanī profectus Pyrenaeōsque montēs circumvectus Emporiīs appulisset clāssem, expositō ibi exercitū, ōrsus ā Lacetānīs omnem ōram usque ad Hibērum flūmen partim renovandīs societātibus, partim novīs īnstituendīs Rōmānae diciōnis fēcit. (Livy xxi. 60.)

While these events were happening in Italy, Cneius Cornelius Scipio had been despatched with a fleet and an army to Spain. He started from the mouth of the Rhone and sailed around the Pyrenees and brought his ships to anchor at Emporiæ. He disembarked his army there, and beginning with the Lacetani, while he renewed old as well as new alliances, he brought under Roman sway the entire coast as far as the river Ebro.

(b) Ipse Hannibal aeger oculīs ex vernā prīmum intemperiē variante calōrēs frīgoraque, elephantō, quī ūnus superfuerat, quō altius ab aquā exstaret, vectus, vigiliīs tamen et nocturnō humōre palustrīque caelō gravante caput, et quia medendī nec locus nec tempus erat, alterō oculō capitur. (Livy xxii. 2.)

Hannibal's eyes suffered from the trying weather of the spring, with its great variations of heat and cold, and therefore he rode on an elephant, which had survived, that he might be as high as possible above the water. Yet long watches, the dews of the night, and the moist climate affected his head: there was neither place nor time for the application of remedies, and the consequence was that he lost one of his eyes.

(c) Inde Tullum Hostilium, nepōtem Hostiliī, cūius in īnfimā arce clāra pūgna adversus Sabīnōs fuerat, rēgem populus iūssit. (i. 22.)

(d) Itaque, ut caedēs manifesta aliquō tamen piāculō luerētur, imperātum patrī, ut fīlium expiāret pecūnia pūblica. Is, quibusdam piāculāribus sacrificiīs factīs, quae deinde gentī Horātiae trāditī sunt, trānsmīssō per viam tigillō, capitē adopertō, velut sub iugum mīsit iuvenem. (i. 26.)

(e) Nocte ūnā audītō perfectōque bellō Sabīnō, posterō diē, in māgnum iam spē undique partae pācis, lēgātī Auruncī senātum adeunt, nī dēcēdātur Volscō agrō bellum indīcantēs. (ii. 26.)

www.ingramcontent.com/pod-product-compliance
Lightning Source LLC
Chambersburg PA
CBHW021513090426
42739CB00007B/589